Who Offended You?

Presented to _____

Date _____

My message to you is _____

_____

_____

_____

_____

_____

Presented by _____

Member of _____

Who Offended You?

Author	Dr. Phillip G. Goudeaux
Cover and Artwork	Scott Cook
Editing	Minister Lue Johnson
	Patricia Fletcher
Graphics	Scott Cook
Publisher	Kenneth L. Sackett Sr.
Typographer	Debra S. Pappas

Published By

Vision Books International
3356A Coffey Lane
Santa Rosa, CA 95403
707-542-1440

Printed In The United States 1994

Who Offended You?

Unlocking Our Hearts to Experience God's Grace

Written By

Dr. Phillip G. Goudeaux

Who Offended You?

Published In The United States Of America
First Printing August 1994

Vision Books International
Kenneth L. Sackett Sr.
Publisher
3356A Coffey Lane
Santa Rosa, CA 95403
707-542-1440

Table Of Contents

	Page
Dedication	vii
Acknowledgements	vii
Preface	viii
Introduction	ix

Part I
Becoming Conscious 11

Reflecting God In Our Hearts 13
Five Keys to Freedom 16

Part II
Satan and the Sower:
Results of His Offenses 21

Satan's Seedy Offenses 23
Trapped By The Weeds 27
Hindered From Receiving The Truth 29
The Enemy Hinders Naaman 31
Naaman—Angry At The Man Of God 36
Offense Against The Church 39
Church Hopping 42
Distracted From The Truth 46
Missing Out On Mighty Works 50
Romantic Love Can Trip Us Up 53
Escalating Offenses 56
Seven Things Satan Loves 58
Making Satan Laugh 59
The Lord Is Not With Us 62

Table Of Contents

Part III
Unlocking Our Hearts 65

It All Begins With A Choice 67
How David Made The Right Choice 68
Choosing Devotion To God 72
Bend Your Ear To God 73
Faith In A Miracle-Working God 76
Put On God's Armor To Remain
   Faithful 79
Recognize What Is Of Real Value 82
But You Can't Please Everyone 84
Discipline Yourself To Be Free
   Of Offense 85

Part IV
Offense-Free For Life! 89

Nine Guidelines For Living Life
   Free From Offense 91
A Daily Prayer 93
Be Blessed, Happy And Fortunate 94

Dedication

This book is dedicated to the glory of **God** and His only begotten son, Jesus Christ, with all my love and thanks for the supernatural power that He has given me as a pastor.

To the staff and membership of Calvary Christian Center, whose faithful prayers and financial support have made this book possible for you to read and pass along to others.

Acknowledgements

I am thankful to God for everyone who has labored so hard to help make this book available for you.

I am also grateful for the loving support of my wife, Brenda, who is always an encouragement to me in every aspect of my life.

And in appreciation for the words of wisdom instilled into my life by my mom, Tanya Craig Chisloms, who has now gone to be with the Lord.

Preface

Holding on to offenses stops many Christians from receiving miracles and breakthroughs in their lives. The first step in dealing with offenses committed against you is to learn how to deal with the offenses you have committed. Married and single people, young and old people, pastors and bill collectors—no one is exempt from offenses.

I desire anyone who holds resentment toward someone else—Christian or non-Christian— to read this book. It could be the answer you need in life.

Dr. Phillip G. Goudeaux

Introduction

I really prayed about this book. I believe God definitely wanted me to write and teach about offenses to help set a lot of people free. The world is full of too many Christians and non-Christians who pull away from jobs, churches, families, marriages, and relationships because it is easier to walk away than it is to talk about their offenses and work things out.

For Christians, breakthroughs are not just going to happen because you want some changes in your life. You've got to start doing something different than what you've been used to doing. This book is going to show you how to have success and give you some key points in this area.

After reading this, your life will never be the same again. This is going to be one of the greatest breakthroughs that has ever happened to you in your life and you won't be able to afford to miss any one of the chapters in this book. Some of you are at home now because somebody offended you, and you'd rather stay home watching the television minister than go and get involved in a church. Someone offended you in the past and you don't want to be involved with anyone else again because you're afraid that they might get you upset. You would rather stay at home and watch church on television and stay in your own comfort zone so that you don't have to deal with other people.

Yet, people can be one of the greatest pleasures of our lives and we are told to love one another as we love ourselves. Let's get back to God, have our hearts renewed and learn to forgive and reach out to our brothers and sisters—offenses and resentments, be gone! And joy and love, here we come! We've got to get down to some real nitty-gritty, nuts-and-bolts ideas because people locked up by offenses and resentments are unable to experience the breakthroughs that God has in store for them.

Part I

Becoming Conscious

Acts 24:16

"And herein do I exercise myself, to have always a conscience void of offence toward God, and toward men."

Reflecting God In Our Hearts

As we try to live and work with others, it is natural as individuals that we will not see eye-to-eye with everyone. However, when we harbor resentments and let ourselves become offended, we are not:

- feeling love and compassion for others;

- being assertive (not aggressive) in stating our needs and feelings;

- trusting God as we turn our hearts and minds toward Him.

Whose heart is perfect towards Him?

God, help us to mature and help us to get our lives to the point where our hearts are perfect.

God is looking for those people whose hearts are perfect towards Him, who are walking free from offense. Have you ever been around people who had been offended? They're bitter, they're mad, they're always talking negatively—especially about the person who offended them.

If we can see the bitterness in others when they harbor resentment, can we also see it in ourselves? Are we brave enough to face our feelings head on, and with God's help (and to the devil's chagrin) become conscious of our pride?

Ask yourself if you are reading this at the right time in your life. Ask if you believe that this book can help you or someone else. Are you ready to learn about tearing down offenses? **The one thing that we need to understand and admit to ourselves is that we are all subject to becoming offended.** If we have a greater understanding of how the enemy comes to offend us, to stop us, then we'll be able to walk in a greater area of victory. We will recognize when the enemy is using us and we must learn how to stop him from hindering us from receiving God's miracles. We can stop him from ripping us off. I believe this is the heart of God, and I feel that this understanding is going to cause people to grow spiritually from where they are in life today to where they want to be.

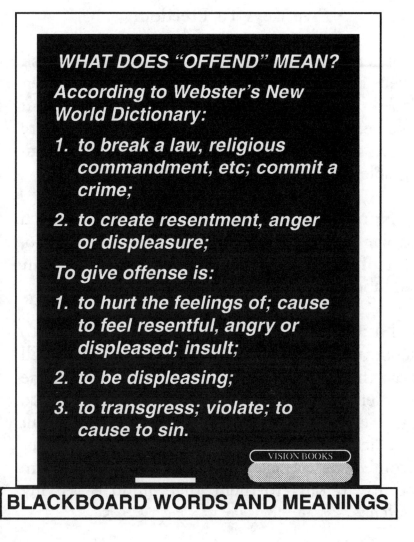

WHAT DOES "OFFEND" MEAN?

According to Webster's New World Dictionary:

1. *to break a law, religious commandment, etc; commit a crime;*

2. *to create resentment, anger or displeasure;*

To give offense is:

1. *to hurt the feelings of; cause to feel resentful, angry or displeased; insult;*

2. *to be displeasing;*

3. *to transgress; violate; to cause to sin.*

VISION BOOKS

BLACKBOARD WORDS AND MEANINGS

Five Keys To Freedom

There are five questions that you need to ask yourself that will indicate whether you've been offended. Most of you probably already know if you've been offended. Do you see how offenses are the devil's tool which he uses to keep you from being able to move forth in God?

Number One: If someone mentions a particular person's name, does it bother you? If so, you are offended. You then say that you don't want to talk about it. Guess what? You're offended!

Number Two: When you're talking to someone who has offended you, is the offense all you can think about? Suppose I went up to someone I had offended a long time ago and started talking to them. I didn't even realize I offended them but they're feeling resentment toward me and never confronted me about it at the time. While I'm innocently talking to them, their mind is reliving the offense.

Number Three: Do you purposely try to avoid people who have offended you? If you do this, then you have been offended. When I'm walking along and see someone who has offended me, and I turn around real fast trying to avoid him—that's how I know I've been offended. What about the holidays? I wonder how many of you reading this have turned down an invitation to go somewhere because you knew so-and-so was going to be there. "Well, I'm not going there because your mama is going to be there. And your mama and I don't get along." The reason why we don't get along is because I got offended. But if I get my own act together our relationship might be on a better footing.

I jog a lot and one day I came upon some little dogs that were sitting by a fence. They were barking and yapping up a storm and it would have been really dumb for me to stop, get on my knees and bark back at them. But when you get offended, you've lowered yourself to the same level of that person, and it's just like lowering yourself to a dog, getting on your knees and barking back at them.

Number Four: Do you spend a great deal of time thinking about someone who has offended you? Then you've been offended. You think about them a lot and you think about what you might say

17

to them when you run into them again. You've been offended.

Number Five: Do you constantly talk about the person who has offended you? Have you ever been around someone who talks about someone else all the time? That person has probably been offended. They're hindered in what they're going to be able to accomplish in their Christian walk because they have been offended.

So now you have five questions that you can ask yourself to determine if you've been offended. One of the greatest areas that the enemy is using today to stop people from being able to go forth in their life is the area of offense. The enemy will try to offend you, to hold you in bondage, to put you in a cage, to stop you from being able to live a bold and victorious life, and stop you from receiving the blessings and the promises that God has for you through Jesus Christ. But if you've been offended, you have allowed yourself to get caught and the enemy is ripping you off . . .

You're wondering why the power of God is not happening in your life. You wonder why your prayers are not being answered. You wonder why you can't get healing in your body. You wonder why you have problems in your marriage. You wonder why you have problems with your finances. It is all because you are walking around with offenses. And satan has you in a cage and is holding you captive. Even as you are reading this now, you are probably thinking that everything is all right, but you can't receive the Word because you're thinking about what somebody did to you. Or you're looking for something to criticize. I'm going to tell you something—you don't have to look for reasons, the devil will give you plenty to choose from.

Part II

Satan and the Sower:
Results of His Offenses

Mark 4:14-17

"The sower soweth the word. And these are they by the way side, where the word is sown; but when they have heard, Satan cometh immediately, and taketh away the word that was sown in their hearts. And these are they likewise which are sown on stony ground; who, when they have heard the word, immediately receive it with gladness; And have no root in themselves, and so endure but for a time: afterward, when affliction or persecution ariseth for the word's sake, immediately they are offended."

Satan's Seedy Offenses

"The sower soweth the word. And these are they by the way side, where the word is sown; but when they have heard, Satan cometh immediately, and taketh away the word that was sown in their hearts."

Mark 4:14-15

If the word of God that is being taught is regarding healing, finances, marriage, children, or God's grace, satan will come immediately to try and rip that word off from you. He knows if you take that word and it gets seeded in your heart, it's going to produce fruit. So, he wants to get the word of God out of you, he wants to steal that word from you because satan knows that the word of God in abundance in you is a powerful weapon against him. What he wants to do is to have you become offended by something so he can rip you off.

A Biblical Study of "Offense"

There are three Hebrew words rendered in the King James version, according to *Unger's Bible Dictionary:*

1. an obstacle or enticement;
2. crime or its penalty;
3. to acknowledge guilt.

Offense also appears to mean that which displeases one; to sin against.

Understand that satan wants to offend us. He wants to pluck us up and stop us from experiencing God's best in our lives. One of the ways he most often does this is through "offending you." When we allow ourselves to get offended, we are no longer able to receive God's best.

In Mark, the fourth chapter, we can look more closely at many offenses to God's work and Word in us. There are those of us who are "beside the road" and are immediately offended by satan, there are those of us who are not firmly rooted and quickly fall away under satan's attacks and there are still others who have heard the Word, yet, through worldly concerns, it is choked out. There are people in the body of Christ who have been offended, therefore allowing the enemy to stop them from receiving God's message. They have allowed satan to hinder (to be behind, to delay) them and keep them from the miracles God has for them.

Satan uses many devices to offend, including trickery to keep us trapped in the feeling of being offended. Being offended cages us and blocks the anointing of God; whether an offense was intentional or unintentional, we become victims of that offense because God has been blocked from speaking to us.

Just because you have heard God's word does not mean it is a part of you. Because you attend church on a regular basis, it does not guarantee you that you will not be vulnerable or that you will not experience offenses. Satan wants to stop you.

Have you ever been to a service where you felt you couldn't hear the messages and said "I hope he (meaning the pastor) leaves me alone. I just came here today to be a good Christian. I don't want him to bother me." You better realize that when this happens you are being ripped off from your miracles. God's Word is falling on deaf ears and is unable to work in your life.

> *"And these are they likewise which are sown on stony ground; who, when they have heard the word, immediately receive it with gladness."* Mark 4:16

Oh alleluia! But wait . . .

> *"And have no root in themselves, and so endure but for a time: afterward, when affliction or persecution ariseth for the word's sake, immediately they are offended."* Mark 4:17

When our gladness becomes poisoned by offenses, God's word can no longer endure in us.

Don't allow people to offend you. All of a sudden someone will say something to you without knowledge of the truth and you will allow them to get you offended. It's called a double whammy. If they can get to you, you can get ripped off. This is when satan attacks.

"And these are they which are sown among thorns; such as hear the word. And the cares of this world, and the deceitfulness of riches, and the lusts of other things entering in, choke the word, and it becometh unfruitful."   Mark 4:18-19

Trapped By The Weeds

A lot of people are not able to go forth in their life because they're trapped by offenses. I was watching an animal show on television that featured a monkey that would put his hand inside a jar to grab a piece of fruit. Well, as long as he held onto the fruit he couldn't pull his hand out of the jar. He would slip his hand in to reach for the fruit and when he'd grab it, he would hold onto it. Instead of letting go of it, he would hold onto it and get ripped off. He was caught, he was snared, he was trapped and wasn't able to go anywhere and all he had to do was turn the offense loose. But instead of turning it loose, he was greedy and he was going to try to hold onto it.

Some of us still have our hands in the jar. All God is asking you to do is turn these things loose.

If you are going to get out of this trap you need to stop allowing the enemy to rip you off. You need to open up your hand and let loose those offenses!

Let me give you a Greek word here, the word is slanderleso where we get our English word slanderous, or slander. It literally means "a part of a trap to which the bait is attached to hinder and to cause to fall." It's an offense that is a deliberately laid trap of the devil. The trap is there to hurt you, to cause you to stumble and to get you or someone else to fall. Slanderleso is what the enemy uses, a trap that he lays, to be able to stop you from going forth in life. How many people have fallen or were hindered because they did not have sense enough to turn the thing loose?

You might think that you have a valid reason for holding onto an offense but the enemy really just has you in a cage. You try to justify your offense against what someone did to you, and you keep bringing those offensive thoughts back up. This makes you feel justified in your feelings and allows you to release your anger. But you're the one in the cage, you are the prisoner.

You have to be smart enough to recognize that the enemy will do anything he can to try to stop you from being victorious and winning in life. He'll do anything he can to try to hinder the power of God from operating through you. Because when you start feeling blessed, and when you start being able to live that bold and victorious life, other people will see what God is doing in your life. It will be a testimony and satan will try even harder to hinder you from being able to move forth in life by offending you.

Satan will use a relative, he'll use your spouse, the boss, your kids, the preacher, anything and anybody he can to try to get you offended. He will try to hurt your feelings, to get you to the point where you'll feel some resentment, or to hold onto some anger or some bitterness in your life so you'll hold onto offenses.

Hindered From Receiving The Truth

In Matthew 11:6 Jesus said, *"And blessed is he, whosoever shall not be offended in me."*

"And blessed—happy, fortunate and to be envied—is he who takes no offense at Me, and finds

29

no cause for stumbling in or through Me, and is not hindered from seeing the Truth."

Matthew 11:6 (Amplified Bible)

So when the enemy gets you offended, he is hindering you from receiving the truth. When I fly on airplanes I use the earplugs to help alleviate the excessive noise, and that is what happens when you get offended. It is like the enemy using anything he can to plug up your ears from being able to receive the truth. You've got earplugs in your ears when you get offended. And that's where a lot of people are in life today. They can be hearing the word of God that can change their lives, but never make any positive changes because they have earplugs in their ears. They can't really hear the truth because they have been offended and are harboring and holding onto that hurt.

Jesus said, *"And blessed is he, whosoever shall not be offended in me."* If people can get offended at Jesus, they can surely get offended at you.

The Enemy Hinders Naaman

Let's now turn to an Old Testament story about Naaman, a Syrian officer whose healing from leprosy was delayed because he became offended.

"Now Naaman, captain of the host of the king of Syria, was a great man with his master, and honourable, because by him the Lord had given deliverance unto Syria; he was also a mighty man in valour, but he was a leper.

"And the Syrians had gone out by companies, and had brought away captive out of the land of Israel a little maid; and she waited on Naaman's wife.

"And she said unto her mistress, 'Would God my lord were with the prophet that is in Samaria! For he would recover him of his leprosy.'

"And one went in, and told his lord, saying, 'Thus and thus said the maid that is of the land of Israel.'

"*And the king of Syria said, 'Go to, go, and I will send a letter unto the king of Israel.' And he departed, and took with him ten talents of silver, and six thousand pieces of gold, and ten changes of raiment.*

"*And he brought the letter to the king of Israel, saying, 'Now when this letter is come unto thee, behold, I have therewith sent Naaman my servant to thee, that thou mayest recover him of his leprosy.'*

"*And it came to pass, when the king of Israel had read the letter, that he rent his clothes, and said, 'Am I God, to kill and to make alive, that this man doth send unto me to recover a man of his leprosy? Wherefore consider, I pray you, and see how he seeketh a quarrel against me.'*

"*And it was so, when Elisha the man of God had heard that the king of Israel had rent his clothes, that he sent to the king, saying, 'Wherefore hast thou rent thy clothes? Let him come now to me, and he shall know that there is a prophet in Israel.'*

"So Naaman came with his horses and with his chariot, and stood at the door of the house of Elisha."   2 Kings 5:1-9

Boy, that really says it—**he stood at the door.** Do you know that there are a lot of folks today that are standing at the door of a miracle. They are standing at the door, they have gone to the right place, they've journeyed to where they need to be, but because they have allowed themselves to get offended, they're still just standing at the door. I wonder what's hindering you from entering through the door to receive your miracle.

"And Elisha sent a messenger unto him, saying, 'Go and wash in Jordan seven times, and thy flesh shall come again to thee, and thou shalt be clean.'" 2 Kings 5:10

But, Naaman became very angry and went away. He thought Elisha, the man of God, would surely come out and call on the name of the Lord his God to cure him of his leprosy.

Up to this point, Naaman did all the right things. This is exactly where a lot of people are in life today. They thought of a good idea, they went to the right place, they did the right things, but they still could not get to where they wanted to be in life because they allowed themselves to get offended.

A Quick Look At Naaman

Naaman served as a high-ranking Syrian officer under King Benhadad of Syria. After stricken with leprosy, he was told of Elisha, the prophet of Israel and man of great healing knowledge.

Upon arriving to Elisha's home in Israel, Naaman sneered at the prophet's instructions to bathe seven times in the Jordan River. Yet when he finally did, his leprosy was cured. Naaman returned to Elisha to give him thanks and even took loads of earth home as a sacrifice to continue to worship the God of Israel.

> *"And Naaman said, 'Shall there not then, I pray thee, be given to thy servant two mules' burden of earth? for thy servant will henceforth offer neither burnt offering nor sacrifice unto other gods, but unto the Lord.'"*　　　　2 Kings 5:17

You can try—you can go to church, you can read your Bible—but if you are holding an offense in you, you are doing nothing but holding back the miracle power of God.

Sometimes people believe that a man of God, a pastor, should do things or see things their way.

They've been called by God. And then they get offended when things don't go the way they think they should. And they still want the blessings of God.

I wonder how many Christians in life today have allowed themselves to be ripped off by the enemy because they thought a man of God did not do something the way they thought it should be done. They are holding onto that offense. It might not be a man of God, it could be a boss. "Well, I thought he should do it this way." Who in the world do they think they are? The enemy has ripped them off and cut off their growth, causing dry rot to enter their life. It doesn't seem to matter how much they reach out to God, or how much they cry out to him, they're not able to get anywhere because they are holding offense in their life.

Naaman initially felt that it should be done a certain way. He felt the man of God should have come out and done his thing, thus healing him. He never had an encounter with a man of God before, but he already had these preconceived ideas about how he thought a man of God should act. Do you know why he acted like this? Because Naaman

35

didn't want to **do** anything to receive his healing. He just wanted immediate healing.

A lot of people today act like this and get offended if God doesn't heal them fast enough. Or they get offended at God because they don't get a breakthrough as fast as they wanted to get it. There is an enemy fighting to try to keep you where you are. You get offended and your faith in what God is able to do has been hindered. You say, "God, I'm doing everything right, where's my healing, my breakthrough?" But you still have that offense in your life. And even though you still do things right, you will not get anywhere if you're holding onto offenses.

Naaman — Angry At The Man Of God

"But Naaman was wroth, and went away, and said, 'Behold, I thought, He will surely come out to me, and stand, and call on the name of the Lord his God, and strike his hand over the place, and recover the leper.'" 2 Kings 5:11

Naaman allowed the enemy, satan, to steal his miracle. He got angry at what the man of God said and then went away in a rage. He was at the door of his miracle, the man of God had already appeared, he had done all the right things, but he allowed himself, at the time he was to receive his miracle, to get angry and offended.

I wonder how many miracles you have allowed the devil to steal out of your life. I wonder how many times God has tried to bring a breakthrough in your life. How many times God has tried to do something in a powerful way. But you allowed your poor attitude to get in the way. What right do we have to get offended at God because we don't get something right away? Or something doesn't go our way?

Naaman was wroth, or very angry, and went away. The man of God had already called him to come and get his miracle, and instead he turned away from his miracle because he allowed himself to get offended.

I wonder if you have allowed the enemy to offend you and cause you to turn away from the miracles that God has for you. Have you left the church or broken off from a marriage relationship because you've gotten offended? Has your child run away because he got offended at you? Do you know that every time you get offended at your parents or at the man of God, you allow an offense to come into your life and you open the door to satan.

A lot of misery is coming into your life not because God made it happen, but because of your stupidity. **You opened the door to the offense.**

Marriages have been broken up, people have lost their jobs, they have not gotten healed and have not gotten their financial breakthroughs because of offenses. People have even died prematurely because of offenses.

Naaman was going in the right direction in his life. He was in need of a miracle, heading to the man of God, and when the man of God said something to him he didn't like, he got offended. He didn't want to go in the muddy waters of the Jordan River, he wanted to go in the river of Ponthias or Pathos where the water was clean. I wouldn't care how the water looked, bless God, if there was a miracle in it; throw me in, in Jesus' name.

Naaman went to the man of God to get his miracle, instead he got offended. This is the biggest problem with a lot of you reading this. You presume all kinds of things and when they don't go your way you're offended. You don't get your healing, you don't get your prayers answered the way you want or fast enough—you're offended.

This happens throughout the entire body of Christ. Many people are offended with God because He hasn't taken care of their situation the way **they presumed** He should.

Once you're offended, the enemy has you in a cage. And here Naaman was, at the brink of his miracle. The Bible said he was at the door ready to receive his miracle, and when the man of God came out and told him what to do he got offended and went away.

Offense Against The Church

Speaking of "going away," why do most people leave a church? Because they get offended. As a pastor of a large church in Sacramento, California, I am amazed when someone gets offended by my teaching. They must think I spend all my time at home on Saturdays thinking of ways to attack them. They think I come to church to get them personally, and that's the farthest thing from my mind. I come to minister to people for God, believing God's word can and will change lives; then someone takes what I say in a personal way and the enemy steps in. When a person feels offended by what is being taught, they stop listening to God's message and become critical.

Have you ever seen those rabbit ear television antennas? What do you put the rabbit ears up for? Better reception. When you get "offended," the rabbit ears go down. Everything is fuzzy and you can't hear clearly any longer. You don't have a picture when the rabbit ears are down.

One of the biggest challenges in the body of Christ stems from people being offended. Remove this "offense" and miracles can happen. People get offended at God or their minister for many reasons, such as not getting their healing as fast as they wanted or not getting a prayer answered. Isn't that crazy to be offended at God? Yet, people still want a blessing in their lives.

*"The sower soweth the word. And these are
they by the way side, where the word is
sown; but when they have heard, Satan
cometh immediately, and taketh away the
word that was sown in their hearts."*

Mark 4:14-15

Right now I'm throwing the Word out to be
sown. Please understand that you have a
responsibility to receive the Word, but satan will
come and try to steal it. Do you realize that an
offense can take the Word of God right out of your
heart; you'll forget that you ever heard it?

After a service one Sunday recently, a woman
came up to me and said, "Excuse me, Pastor. Do
you have a word from God for me?" I just taught a
whole hour and she wanted to know if I had a word
from God for her. All those words that God spoke
through me that whole hour and she wants a word
now? So I said, "Excuse me one second. Yes, yes I
am getting a word from God. The Lord said, '**Read
your Bible.**'" Naturally she got offended.

However, the greatest word or advice you can
ever receive is "Read your Bible." As Christians, we
don't need to go running around looking for a

41

Word from God for someone to give us. Read the Word. He'll expose us to His truth which we need in our lives.

Church Hopping

There are Christians who don't want to be exposed to the truth in their lives. When they get offended in church, they quit and go somewhere else. But you can't just take your old, unhappy, offended self and go over to another church and expect a change just because you left. It doesn't make any difference where you go; as long as you are holding onto that offense you're never going to be set free, and Jesus will never be able to do anything in your life. You need to get it corrected before you leave the church where the offense occurred.

When people come to me and say, "I left my church because my pastor said this, or my pastor said that . . ." I tell them to return to their church and get it right with the pastor. I don't want people coming here offended. They'll do nothing but infect others. They must get it right with their pastor first. Churches like to say they're independent, but we need to try to get all the independents to be more dependent upon one another. I believe that when someone leaves a church they need to leave in good standing. If they don't leave in good standing, other pastors should not accept them into their church no matter how badly they want a new member. If pastors allow someone who is offended to come into their church, they're doing nothing but allowing a plague to enter.

If a person is holding onto offensive baggage, they're always ready to attack. I've had people get offended at my youth minister. Can you believe it? Offended at the youth minister? I've had people get offended by the music at my church. The music is either too loud, or it's not loud enough. I've had people get offended because at the end of the service we play the music. They say you shouldn't play music at the end of the service.

One Sunday my wife wore a pink dress to service. I thought it looked great on her. She's always dressing for me, for our children, and to look her best for God, as well as the church. But a woman came up and told her she didn't like her in a pink dress. Well, that offended me, this woman isn't paying our bills. I like the way my wife dresses. One corner of her closet is filled with dresses that people told her they didn't like. I finally said to her, "Honey, don't you let anybody tell you what to wear. If I like it and you bought it because you liked it, then you wear it." Be honest, would you be offended at this? Of course you would! But remember who's behind the offense. We didn't get upset with these people, we just prayed for them.

No matter what you do, somebody is going to get offended. If you can't please them, they get offended. You would be surprised at how people will get offended at anything. I've had people say the following: "I'm going away because the music is too loud"; or "They don't have enough whites in the choir"; or "They don't have enough whites on staff." People will find anything at which to get offended if they allow satan to set them up for it. If there's not enough men in the choir and you're a man, get in the choir. Then you'll hear, "Well, I can't sing." Well, we'll teach you. If you think that there is not sexual or racial balance and you're offended by it, see if you can change it. The point is—**get involved without offense.**

I had a man leave the church because I allowed mixed marriages in the church. Blacks and whites or Hispanics and whites or Japanese and Chinese to blacks or whites. I had a man tell me that if I allowed this to continue in my church, he was leaving the church. He got offended. Offended at people he didn't even know because they were married, in his opinion, to the wrong colors.

One afternoon I was witnessing to a woman at a hospital and I asked her to come to Calvary Christian Center. She said, "Oh, nobody lets me come to their church." I asked her why not and she said, "Because I'm married to a black man and nobody wants me in their church." I told her to come to Calvary, that we'd love her. **Jesus is not hung up on color.** But people, through the devil, will do all kinds of things to get you to think Jesus is racist. Do you understand what I'm stating? People get offended at any little incident.

> *"And it came to pass, that when Jesus had finished these parables, he departed thence. And when he was come into his own country, he taught them in their synagogue, insomuch that they were astonished, and said, 'Whence hath this man this wisdom, and these mighty works? Is not this the carpenter's son?'"*
>
> Matthew 13:53-55

Distracted From The Truth

As told in Matthew 13, the people in Jesus' own homeland came to see what God was trying to tell them. Instead of looking and receiving what God had for them, they looked at the man and began to get offended.

> *"Is not this the **carpenter's son?** is not his mother called Mary? and his brethren, James, and Joses, and Simon, and Judas?"*
>
> Matthew 13:55

> *"And his sisters, are they not all with us? Whence then hath this man all these things?"*   Matthew 13:56

> *"And they were offended in him."*
>
> Matthew 13:57

He was there blessing them, trying to help them and all that they could do was to analyze him and try to find fault in him. What were they analyzing? Who His mother was! What did His mother have to do with the mighty works? What

46

did His mother have to do with what He was teaching them? They got offended because of an unimportant matter.

As Jesus was ministering the Word of God, Matthew says that the people were astonished at the anointing and the power of God that was in His life. Matthew goes on to comment about the wisdom that came from Him, and that the people were astonished at the power of God and the mighty works that He did. Here was Jesus, the miracle worker, the power of God in their presence, and they were astonished at the anointing. They were amazed at His wisdom and at the mighty works that He did. And then they started tearing Him apart, asking, **"Don't we know Him? Don't we know His mama? Don't we know His brothers and His sisters? Didn't He work in the carpenter's shop?"** And the Bible says that they were offended.

We can get offended at some of the stupidest things. What did His mama, His brothers and sisters, and His working in the carpenter's shop have to do with the power and presence of God that was there to give them their miracle? Anytime the enemy can get us sidetracked, or can get us looking off in a different direction, he'll do it. Why? Because

47

you are a danger to the enemy when you can walk free from offenses. When you can keep yourself from being hurt, you are a danger to the enemy.

"Isn't that the little colored boy who used to live on the skid street? Didn't we know him when . . . ? Didn't he used to run around here and get into trouble when he was a kid? Wasn't he in the Black Panther party? Didn't I see him in jail one time?" People get offended at you about things that happened twenty to thirty years in your past. I've been saved twenty years and old acquaintances are still looking at my past. They can recall your mother, or where you went to school, or something you did that was wrong.

Not too long ago, I had a couple come up to me at one of my services right after they joined my ministry. The man came up to me and said, "Oh, we love the Word here, we like the way you have things organized, and we like the power of God that is in your church." This couple was telling me all kinds of things and then all of a sudden the man said, "Didn't you go to City College?" And I said, "Yes, I did." He said, "Weren't you involved in the Black Panther party?" I said, "Yeah!" Then he said, "Well, didn't you used to hang around so-and-so?" I said, "Yeah!" Then more questions about my past came one after another. This happened the day they joined the church and since then they have not been back. They were offended about my past. But all I can say is **"He that is without sin, cast the first stone."** Who has had a perfect past? Who has not messed up somewhere along the line? And if you think that you have got it all together, then that's where you are the biggest offender.

I had an acquaintance at church who used to be one of the guys I boxed with in a gym. His wife was saved at my church. This man was big and strong, and I used to win the match with him when we were kids. But he let me know one day that he was ready for a real fight. He said his wife was saved and he grabbed my hand and squeezed so hard that it felt like the bones were breaking. At first I thought he was squeezing it in a friendly way, but then he wouldn't turn my hand loose. There wasn't anyone around to help either. I thought my hand was broken; he just stared at me and kept squeezing my hand. He was offended that his wife was saved and that she was trying to bring him to accountability.

However, her efforts didn't work and he ended up in prison where he still is today. He's there because something offended him and the enemy held him in bondage. He was offended because either his wife was saved, or offended in the way that God was using me. How unfortunate that the enemy has held him in a prison cage ever since. You know what is so sad? He's in a literal cage and there's a lot of people in life today that are held in spiritual cages where their spirit is in bondage with the devil because they hold onto offenses of their past.

Missing Out On Mighty Works

"And they were offended in him. But Jesus said unto them, 'A prophet is not without honor, save in his own country, and in his own house.'" Matthew 13:57

*"And he did **not** many mighty works there because of their unbelief."* Matthew 13:58

This is such a sad part: *"And he did not many mighty works **there**"* because they were in their offenses **there**. He couldn't do many mighty works

there. I wonder, are you **there**? Because if you are in the land of the **there**, that's where the enemy has you in bondage and because you are **there**, Jesus can't do many mighty works in your life.

This is a key point because this is where the son of God was. The miracle worker himself was in their presence to perform a miracle. God had brought a miracle worker in their presence to perform miracles for them, but they could not receive the miracle because they were so busy looking at the person.

> *"Is this not the carpenter's son? Is not his mother called Mary? And his brethren, James, and Joses, and Simon, and Judas? And his sisters, are they not all with us? Whence then hath this man all these things? And they were offended in him. But Jesus said unto them, 'A prophet is not without honor, save in his own country, and in his own house.'"* Matthew 13:55-57

It might have been an ex-husband that offended you or it might have been an ex-boss, or an ex-wife. It might have been something that happened to you that was terrible or painful; maybe you were raped, molested, or witnessed something bad happening to someone you loved. The enemy is holding you **there**, where Jesus won't be able to do mighty works in or through you. Satan has you trapped **there** because you refuse to let go. Jesus can't do many mighty works in your life until you're ready to give up the offense or the hurt and pain.

The problem today is that there are a lot of Christians that are never going to accomplish much in their lives because they're staying asleep in church. The enemy has held them in the land of **there**. What I need to impress upon you is that I don't care what someone has done to you, or what has happened to you, or whatever offense you're holding onto, you cannot allow yourself to stay **there**. You cannot afford to let the enemy hold you **there** because when you are **there**, the enemy has you where he wants you, and Jesus cannot come in and do his mighty works. Why? Because you have not come clean with your offenses. This was the son of God, as told in Matthew, the power of God was upon him. He did miracles and wonders everywhere he went. But because they were **there**, because they were offended, because they held onto something that happened to them in the past, because they held onto those offenses, they were **there**. Jesus cannot do anything for you until you stop hanging onto offenses.

We need to hear the voice of God to help us move from where we are to where we want to be.

Romantic Love Can Trip Us Up

Love and marriage carries its own baggage of problems that can lead to destructive resentments and offenses. In my teachings, I've made mention about men and women living together out of wedlock. This is not a popular subject in the church. I don't say this to offend anyone in particular, but in God's eyes we know it's wrong. Yet, it seems like it's a popular thing to do these days because people don't want to make the commitment to get married.

Once, after I spoke of commitment, a woman came up to me and said, "You have cut me; you have cut me real deep and I am bleeding all inside; you almost killed me." And I said to her, "I'm sorry that I didn't. Because when you die to the flesh, then Christ can start living." She wasn't prepared for that. God wanted to bring her into accountability with Him so that she could have a breakthrough of insight. However, she wasn't ready to give up her comfort zone to have a closer fellowship with God. Instead, she was offended, therefore, ripped off and God could not help her. This woman had a problem with commitment and was living in sin. Yet when she heard the truth, she became offended.

Please understand that I am not advocating that you just jump into marriage in order to make a commitment. I'm always telling people not to just jump up and marry someone just because they think they're in love. "You love them?" I ask. "Well, how long have you known them? Two days? You don't love them—you **lust** them." There's no love in that. Another word for lust is desire.

I didn't just jump up and marry; I took my time to get to know my wife. I thank God that she is going to be the only woman I'll ever be with until Jesus comes back. Before making such commitments, you've got to sit down and talk to that person. You've got to talk, and talk, and talk.

I wish that some couples who want to get married could never see one another and instead just talk to each other over the phone. You don't need to be together all the time mainly because you can't keep your hands off one another. You can have a relationship without touching and without kissing. You just need to become saved, to become redeemed.

So you think you are in love and then you get married. Three weeks later you're thinking, "I made a mistake." Yes, you did. You made a mistake because you didn't get to know one another. You don't jump into a relationship because the person looks good, or has a good job. You need to know what's in their head and what's in their heart. You need to know what's in their heart because when you get married, God says it is until death do you part.

If you do not know the person you are marrying, you are setting yourself up for terrible misunderstandings, resentments and offenses. People are having problems because they get married and then the other person does something to offend them. They get offended because they're both immature and don't know one another. Once you get offended, your ears are open to the devil and he's speaking in your life. This will destroy the best of marriages and lead to divorce.

Divorce and remarriage has its own set of problems as well. Beware of someone who has been married before and is carrying offenses from their prior marriage. If they're carrying all these offenses, they'll bring them into the new marriage and soon you will be the one victimized over something that happened to them from their past failed marriage. God can't really bless a new marriage if a person is entering into that marriage offended. So make sure before you get married that your divorced and soon-to-be spouse has it all together (or is seriously working their way toward such a goal). If they have lots of hang-ups, if they have lots of problems, then they're going to bring their offenses against you, like it or not. The offense will escalate and Jesus won't do any mighty works in your life or in your marriage.

Escalating Offenses

When you open the door to offenses, be it in marriage, work relationships, or your walk with God, the enemy will tag along, inviting other demons and spirits to jump on your back and pretty soon they'll just wear you down. You can slowly, unknowingly become a pack mule for offensive baggage. I say unknowingly because you may not know it when it happens. It doesn't happen instantly; the enemy starts by dry-rotting your roots. How? Because you allowed yourself to get offended; you allowed some insignificant thing to affect you.

Another analogy from our animal kingdom comes to mind: this one is about buzzards. You become nothing but a buzzard when you've been offended because you start picking the person apart who has offended you. You start justifying your offense by finding fault in them. You blame them for the situation you are in and then you start to pick them apart. One thing about a buzzard is that it likes to rip meat apart. It has a special stomach and can eat really spoiled meat, rotten meat. When you become a buzzard, you just start ripping people and your mouth becomes spoiled and rotten. You're just spoiling yourself; you're taking that bitterness into your life even more. You're pulling more filth into your life because you got offended.

There are many unhappy, resentful, spoiled people in this country. Maybe if the country came back to God things would start working out for people. Do you know that there are people who are trying to take "In God we Trust" off of the dollar bill? There are many who are working in all kinds of ways to keep prayer out of the schools, out of ceremony rites, and out of a lot of other things.

There is no one that is going to be able to lead this country or make this country great again until we get back to God. Nothing is going to work until then. Not until the saints of God learn how to start praying instead of being offended.

Seven Things Satan Loves

"These six things doth the Lord hate; yea, seven are an abomination unto him: A proud look, a lying tongue, and hands that shed innocent blood, An heart that deviseth wicked imaginations, feet that be swift in running to mischief, A false witness that speaketh lies, and he that soweth discord among brethren."

Proverbs 6:16

With the exception of shedding innocent blood, much of what the Lord calls abominations have to do with our slanderous words against our neighbor. If you're dumb enough to listen to what someone else has to say that is negative about

58

somebody, then you're just as bad as they are. Some people will be offended at what someone said about somebody else. That's why I never tell my wife if someone does something bad to me. I never tell her about such things because she loves me and she will automatically take my side in the matter. I don't want her running around offended or being mad at someone because of what they said about me. It can be a double whammy. The devil has us both in a bag because I'm offended and she's offended too. He's got both of us. And if she tells someone else, then they might get offended. The devil wants to keep us running our mouths, and then he wants to include people dumb enough to listen to us.

Making Satan Laugh

Offenses can teach us some lessons. Think a minute and ask yourself if, because of offenses, you have been ripped off from: your potential, from God's truth for your life, from enjoying people, even enjoying church, from reaching what God has for you in your life? The enemy is sitting back laughing at you, and saying, "Oh, isn't he dumb to hold onto those things that somebody did to him."

Sometimes we hold an offense against someone and they are not even aware of it. They are not affected by it at all. If they're not aware of or affected by it, it doesn't make sense to be offended. In situations like this, it makes us look dumb and no one likes being a dummy. But if we are unhappy over something that someone said or did and they don't know it, what good can come out of it? In every way imaginable it's a waste and is destructive. Our time, thoughts, and health can be destroyed by holding onto offenses. Even worse than that, your walk with God is hindered.

I have been a dummy. I have let people pull my strings. I have allowed people to offend me and to hurt me. I have held onto some things and let the enemy rip me off until God opened up my eyes and said, "Don't you allow the enemy to operate in you like that. He's stealing My Word from you. Satan is stealing your blessings from you because you allowed someone to get to you for whatever reason." I'm trying to do my best, to do good, and get people to love the Lord. God had to open me up to see that I was allowing offenses to separate me from being a good shepherd. I had to face reality and see the truth.

Some people are offended by a multitude of things. As a pastor, I have seen many people become offended at my teachings, such as on the subject of walking in divine health, or receiving healing. The enemy is going to try to steal that from you by offending you sometime. Maybe you don't believe that, but you have to realize that you're not the sum total of all knowledge. We don't know it all. Thank God I still have a lot to learn. And I'm not ashamed in admitting that I'm still learning. But the problem is when somebody says, "Well, I don't agree with that." Right then the enemy is stealing the Word from them. He has jumped at the chance when someone starts disagreeing before they have considered the truth and think that they have already got it together. It starts at the point when they say, "I don't like what he said" without giving the subject much consideration at all. That's where the enemy starts working on offending.

This doesn't have to be solely with the pastor. It could be with someone else. The enemy works in all kinds of ways; he'll use anything he can to knock a stumbling block in front of you. The enemy wants God's Word from you. I find it hard enough to teach something that I know will challenge people, but I know that I've got to teach them because

God's Word says, **"And the truth,"** not denominationalism, not manisms but **"The truth shall set you free."**

The Lord Is Not With Us

Our offenses and resentments have one more final devastating result. We may have hurt our neighbors, our spouses and ourselves (not to mention pleased satan immensely), but when we become offended, we have angered our Lord. God says,

"I will go and return to my place, till they acknowledge their offence, and seek my face: in their affliction they will seek me early." Hosea 5:15

Do you know what God has just said in that passage? He has said that He will leave from your presence because you are holding onto an offense. He said He doesn't even want to be around you until you get it right. That's what the Bible says.

You wonder why sometimes things aren't happening for you. You feel that God hasn't heard your prayers and some things don't feel right. It is because you are holding onto offenses. Do you know why God doesn't want to be "around" you? It is because when you get offended you have given your ear to the devil. When you open your door to an offense, when you allow yourself to be dumb enough to receive an offense, God said that the enemy now has your ear. Satan has your ear and he will continually bombard you with all kinds of reasons why you need to stay offended. He will hold you in bondage as long as you allow him to take your ear. And God says, I don't want to have anything to do with you until you acknowledge your offense, until you get smart enough to do something about the position you are in. God said, I'm going to get away from you.

What can we do to overcome resentments and stop becoming offended? God has shown us a way . . .

Part III

Unlocking Our Hearts

II Chronicles 16:9

"For the eyes of the Lord run to and fro throughout the whole earth, to shew himself strong in the behalf of them whose heart is perfect toward Him."

It All Begins With A Choice

You have to make a choice and that choice is either to live in your offenses and stay miserable for the rest of your life or to be able to cast them away and walk free from offenses. The Lord said,

> *"Cast your cares, your anxieties, your burdens, cast them on the Lord for he cares for you."*

You weren't made to carry offenses. You weren't made to carry that kind of burden, or to hold onto that kind of anger, hate and bitterness in your life. You inherently don't want to allow something to rip you off from what God has for you because of your own lack of sensitivity or lack of response to what the Word of God has to say. Don't allow the enemy to cheat you out of life's blessings. All of us can stand an extra blessing. We all need God's miracles in our lives.

> *"Who was delivered for our offences, and was raised again for our justification."*
> Romans 4:25

We don't have to carry the offenses because Jesus already delivered us from them. You've got to make the decision to either hold onto them or let them go. You're the one who has to make the decision.

Do you know that sometimes we'll fight to stay wrong. Just like the monkey that would get his hand stuck in the jar and wouldn't turn the piece of fruit loose. He was fighting to stay wrong, a captive held because he wouldn't turn the thing loose. Here is our choice: to remain captives or to walk free. We **can** walk free once we choose to do so; it is possible to live a life of love and compassion toward those around us, freeing ourselves of resentments that destroy.

How David Made The Right Choice

Now, you all know the story about David the shepherd and how he was watching over his father's sheep when there was a supposed war going on. There really was no war, just Goliath bullying the Israelite soldiers who were afraid of what the giant was going to do to them. So, here was David bringing lunch to his brother.

"And Eliab his eldest brother heard when he spake unto the men; and Eliab's anger was kindled against David, and he said, 'Why camest thou down hither? and with whom hast thou left those few sheep in the wilderness? I know thy pride, and the naughtiness of thine heart; for thou art come down that thou mightest see the battle.'"
1 Samuel 17:28

Do you know what he was saying to him? He was saying, "You little jive-turkey, what are you doing here? You know better than this. You're suppose to be tending the sheep. You do not have any right to be here." David came to bring his brother lunch and instead he got chewed out. He came to bring lunch but God had a miracle in store for him. David was trying to do a good thing but Eliab, his brother, came against him and started speaking harshly to him. At that point, David could have allowed Eliab's attitude to get to him and if he had, he never would have killed his giant.

Ready—Aim—Fire

David chose not to allow himself to become resentful toward his elder brother despite his condemning remarks. Instead, he went on to fight and slay the giant. What are the giants in your life? Here are some you may find super-sized:

- Bitterness
- Anger
- Resentment
- Jealousy
- Pride
- Lust

Ready? Aim and Fire!

Have you ever had somebody talk badly about you when you were trying to do something good? There are a lot of giants that will come against you in your life that you need to kill. But you will never kill your giants until you make a decision not to be offended. You will never be able to walk in victory until you make the decision that you're not going to be offended; you're not going to allow people to get to you. You are not going to turn away from that miracle that God has for you. Samuel says that when Eliab spoke as he did to David, had the little brother been offended he would never have killed Goliath. You will never kill the giants in your life until you make the decision not to be offended.

David had a choice to either allow himself to get an attitude, like a lot of people would have done, or to step over the offense.

Oh, thank God today that some people, when they're given the opportunity to get offended, they just step over it. Every time the enemy comes against them, they just step over it. Every time you step over an offense, you are, at that time, ready to receive your miracle and kill the giant that is coming against you in Jesus' name. But you've got to be willing to step over those offenses. You have to be willing to step over the stupidities of some people. You've got to be willing to act instead of just sitting around harboring the offense.

David listened to Eliab's condemning remarks **but he paid no attention to him.** You're never going to walk in victory until you start stepping over offenses. No one is perfect. No one has it all together. And I don't care what it is that they do to you; if it's your spouse or whoever, you cannot allow yourself to get offended.

Choosing Devotion To God

"For the eyes of the Lord run to and fro throughout the whole earth, to shew himself strong in the behalf of them whose heart is perfect toward him."

2 Chronicles 16:9

God is trying to show himself strong on the behalf of those whose hearts are perfect. Perfect? Impossible you say? It is true that we cannot have **perfect** hearts toward God—we are sinners. In this context, "perfect" is closer to the meaning of being mature, devoted and committed to Him.

There are going to be wars and there are going to be challenges that will come into your life. But you have stopped God from being able to act on your behalf because you were foolish enough to hold onto an offense. You allowed a hurt or a pain to just harbor in your life. Yes, it will come, but you need to let it hit you and then bounce off. You don't have to hold onto things. Say "No, I don't accept that pain, I'm not going to accept that offense. I'm not going to allow that person to get to me." Whatever they say or do, release it, let it go in Jesus' name. When you are able to turn offenses loose, regardless of what the offense is, then you are mature and devoted to the body of Christ. How can we begin to have "perfect" hearts? We must first make the choice to listen to God.

Bend Your Ear To God

"My son, attend to my words; incline thine ear unto my sayings." Proverbs 4:20

God says, I want you to bend your ear towards My Word. You've got to make the decision, you have a choice, and that is to allow yourself to hear the Word. You can choose not to, God isn't going to **make** you receive the Word; it is your choice to make.

When I was in elementary school, there was a woman who was the principal and I remember her as being very mean. Those were the days when we had corporal punishment in school and you didn't say or do one thing out of line; you didn't even *look* funny because the teachers would punish you. I

73

remember one time, I don't remember what I did, but the principal grabbed my ear and strutted me down the hallway all the way to the office. She took me into her office and spanked me good for something I can't even remember now. Glory to God.

God says, *"I want your ear, I want you to bend your ear."*

Proverbs advises, *"My son, attend to my words; incline thine ear unto my sayings."*

Verse 21 of Proverbs 4 says, *"Let them not depart from thine eyes; keep them in the midst of thine heart."*

This is the choice you have. Satan will immediately come to take the Word from you through persecutions or through afflictions.

Attend

The meaning of "attend" as used in Proverbs 4:20, *"attend to My words"* is:

— "to pay attention to; give heed;
— "to be in **readiness**; wait upon;
— "to devote or apply oneself to; to give the required care or attention"

(Webster's New World Dictionary)

By now you know that offenses are the number one tool that the devil uses to stop people from being able to go forth in God. Offenses are the wall that stops most Christians from being able to operate in the spirit of God. Offenses stop you from being able to receive from God. Offenses are the number one reason that people run away from the church. These people leave bearing the offenses of how they're feeling. The enemy uses offenses within the church, and also in other areas of your life.

People who are in bondage are going through all kinds of challenges in their life. Why? Because they've been offended. Satan will use offenses to pluck you out. He'll use something to get to you, perhaps something that someone says or something that they do. He will try to stop you from being able to live a bold and victorious and overcoming Christian life. He wants you to believe that there is never any victory, only problems.

We are told over and over that the path to salvation and victory is to lose our lives to Jesus Christ. We need to forget ourselves, turn down the noise, and bend an ever-attentive ear toward God. If you could set your feelings *outside* yourself, it would enable you to be able to receive what God can do for you *inside* your life.

Faith In A Miracle-Working God

Ask yourself if you believe that God is a miracle-working God. Do you believe He is Elshadi, the God who is More Than Enough; that He is Elohim, the God of Miracles?

> *"Therefore I say unto you, 'What things soever ye desire, when ye pray, believe that ye receive them, and ye shall have them.'"*
> Mark 11:24

Oh, don't we like that! I know that scripture backwards and forwards. Whatever you desire when you pray, believe that you will receive it and you shall have it. Believe that you will receive it and you shall have it.

In the case of resentments and being offended, you need to believe that your heart can be healed and you will receive from God. Why? Because God wants to be back in your presence and He wants you to love your neighbor.

God said, *"forgive . . ."* God says that until you acknowledge your offenses, nothing will happen for you. Remember, He said, *". . . unto you, 'What things soever ye desire, when ye pray, believe that ye receive them, and ye shall have them.'"*

> *"And when ye stand praying, forgive, if ye have ought against any; that your Father also which is in heaven may forgive you your trespasses. But if ye do not forgive, neither will your Father which is in heaven forgive your trespasses."*
>
> Mark 11:25-26

That's strong. And I'm going to tell you, when you stand praying, forgive. He said that your Father, also which is in heaven, may forgive you your trespasses. And that's the biggest thing that hinders the body of Christ from receiving the blessings that God has for us.

Jesus came to save the world. When He was on the cross you'd think people would have been there to help Him. Can you imagine what Jesus had to deal with? He hung on that cross and the very ones that hollered out "crucify him," still had fish and bread crumbs on their mouths. They had just gotten through eating the miracle lunch. They had been there and received healing from Him, and had been there when all the power of God was in operation. Can you believe that they were the same ones who crucified Him? Can you imagine how they hurt the son of God? And how He felt on the cross when the people were mocking him? But do you know what was foremost in Jesus' mind? He wanted to make sure that He didn't go to heaven with an offense. He said, *"Father, forgive them, for they know not what they do."*

When an offense comes against you, you need to just throw your hands up and say, "I'm not going to receive that offense. I'm not going to allow it to stop me. Father, forgive them, for they don't know what they are doing."

Put On God's Armor To Remain Faithful

"Finally, my brethren, be strong in the Lord, and in the power of his might. Put on the whole armour of God, that ye may be able to stand against the wiles of the devil. For we wrestle not against flesh and blood, but against principalities, against powers, against the rulers of the darkness of this world, against spiritual wickedness in high places. Wherefore take unto you the whole armour of God, that ye may be able to withstand in the evil day, and having done all, to stand. Stand therefore, having your loins girt about with truth, and having on the breastplate of righteousness; And your feet shod with the preparation of the gospel of peace; Above all, taking the shield of faith, wherewith ye shall be able to quench all the fiery darts of the wicked. And take the helmet of salvation, and the sword of the Spirit, which is the word of God." Ephesians 6:10-17

I believe that God's helmet of salvation has ear muffs to stifle all the offenses people throw at us. Remember, you're the temple of God and **Jesus is Lord!**

Don't allow the Word to be taken from you. You always have to guard your attitude. You need to "Keep (God's Word) in the midst of thine heart," as we've already seen that Proverbs 4:21 instructs us. The word *keep* is a military term and it means to guard as a soldier would guard an installation. So *keep* means to guard or protect the Word. One of the duties in a military operation is guard duty. When a person is on guard duty his job is that of protection and if he fails in his responsibilities it could mean severe punishment for him. Why? Because he did not protect what he had been given to guard or to keep.

God is telling us that we have the same responsibility—we have to guard and protect. The majority of the words that God gives us have to do with life and death. Because the enemy is ripping off Christians, they have never attained a position in their lives where they have been able to receive the abundance that God has for them. They have never been able to rise to that spiritual level where they can have that sweet communion with the Holy Spirit.

> *"For (My words) are life unto those that find them, and health to all their flesh."*
>
> Proverbs 4:22

The Word of God equals life. Do you see why the enemy tries so hard to offend you and stop you from receiving the Word—**because the Word is life.**

> *". . . the words that I speak unto you, they are spirit, and they are life."* John 6:63

Jesus said, *"My word is spirit and my word is life. The more I receive the word, the more I'm able to protect it, and guard it, and keep it inside of me, and the more life is going to permeate out of me."*

> *"For they are life unto those that find them, and health to all their flesh. Keep thy heart with all diligence; for out of it are the issues of life."* Proverbs 4:22-23

Keep your heart, that Word that has been given to you. Don't allow the enemy to offend you and rip off the Word that God has given you. He has given life and health to all your flesh.

Recognize What Is Of Real Value

"And this I pray, that your love may abound yet more and more and extend to its fullest development in knowledge and all keen insight . . . so that you may surely learn to sense what is vital, and approve and prize what is excellent and of real value—recognizing the highest and the best, and distinguishing the moral differences; and that you may be untainted and pure and unerring and blameless, that—with hearts sincere and certain and unsullied—you may [approach] the day of Christ, not stumbling nor causing others to stumble." Philippians 1:9-11 (Amplified Bible)

I'm going to share a somewhat embarrassing personal story with you that could have been a chance for me to become offended. I was getting ready to go to a party with a friend of mine. I had been saved for twenty years and this happened twenty-three years ago. I was getting ready for the party and I had just brushed my teeth and gargled with some mouthwash. Now you know that mouthwash will kill a million germs, besides feeling like it burns all your gums. After finishing with that, I got into the car with my friend and he handed me some breath mints. I said to him, "No, thank you, I don't need them." He said, "Here are some mints," and I said, "I don't need them, no thank you." He said, "You don't understand, here are some mints, take them." And I said, "I don't want any. Do you understand?" He said, "Listen to me, your breath stinks, take some mints. Remember when we went out the other night with those girls? One of them said your breath stinks." I said, "Give me all the mints. I'll take them, I'll take them all."

I could have gotten offended and said, "Let me out. Don't you talk to me like that. Don't tell me about my breath." I could have done what most people would do and say to myself, "He shouldn't have said that." I could have gotten offended and never received what he had to say. But do you know what? When he said what he did, it made me realize I might have a problem with gum disease so I went to the dentist. I went and did something about it. Sometimes people will say something to us trying to help us out, yet we will get our feelings hurt and never make progress from where you are, to where we should be.

But You Can't Please Everyone

As you go through life, people are going to offend you. Not everyone is going to like you. Everyone won't appreciate your love for God or your zeal to live righteously. Not everyone will understand your intentions all of the time. Your attitude towards these people should be—so what! They didn't understand Jesus and Jesus lived without offense.

I've been a pastor for twelve years. I have had people get offended in many areas. They've been offended at my wife over what she does or doesn't wear, and what she does or doesn't do. I've had people get offended at the music ministry, what they sing or what they don't sing and over how loud the music should be. I mean, at times, it is just a no-win situation. People get offended in all kind of areas. They've been offended at people because they clap or they dance in church. I've had people get offended because somebody got up and just started worshipping the Lord.

People get offended at what kind of car I drive. I'll be honest, I drive a Mercedes-Benz. "Do you know he's got a Mercedes and he's a preacher," people scoff. Well, show me in the Bible where it says a preacher can't have a Mercedes. In fact, some of you ministers who are reading this book need to get loosened up and realize that God wants the best for his people. You need to raise your sights and come to the area where God can bless you. But the point is, you won't be able to please everyone—someone may become offended at your actions. Look to God as the one to please and rather than becoming offended yourself, have compassion, show forgiveness and put on the armor of God's word. You'll be blessed!

Discipline Yourself To Be Free Of Offense

> *"Therefore I always exercise and discipline myself—mortifying my body [deadening my carnal affections, bodily appetites and worldly desires], endeavoring in all respects—to have a clear (unshakable, blameless) conscience, void of offense toward God and toward men."*
>
> Acts 24:16 Amplified Bible

Acts 24 is one of the most important messages to be taught if we're going to walk in our miracles. Paul says he wants to have his mind free and clear from any offense. He says, "void and unshakable, blameless." He doesn't want to let anything or anybody get to him who will rip him off and stop him from receiving his miracle. He won't allow anything in his life that would open the door for the devil to rip him off.

Daily Do's For Spiritual Fitness

- Set aside quality time to read God's Word.
- Pray and meditate in solitude.
- Admit your wrongs, offenses and resentments and ask for forgiveness.
- Listen carefully for God's special message to you.

I'm glad that my heart is committed to walk free from offense. Recently I was at home praying and the spirit of God spoke to me and said "Have you really checked yourself out lately? You're holding onto some offenses in your life." I said, "Not me, God." I started thinking about some people who did some things to me in the past and when I thought about them I realized that they did get to me. Well, God brought them back to me then and said, "Remember the question of being offended when someone's name is mentioned? Or the question of talking about someone constantly?" I just fell on my face and cried out to God to forgive me for holding onto any offenses.

"And herein do I exercise myself." Acts 24:16

Let's stop right here for a minute. Remember that no one can exercise for you. Is that a deep revelation? How many of you wish that someone could exercise for you? God, please let them do those sit-ups for me. Let them run for me and tighten my muscles. But, no one can exercise for you and no one can get rid of your offenses but you.

Do what it says in Acts 24:16. Always exercise and discipline yourself, mortifying your body, deadening your carnal affections, your body appetites and worldly desires, and endeavoring in all respects to have a clean, unshakable, blameless, conscious void of offenses towards God and towards men.

Paul says, *"I'm going to make one thing clear. I'm going to work real hard at keeping myself from*

being offended and allowing the devil to rip me off.
I'm going to try really hard."

I declare my liberty today in Jesus' name. I'm free from offenses. Glory to God. I'm like Paul, I exercise myself from this day forth so that I will be free from offenses toward God and toward men in Jesus' name. You can't do this alone; you need the power of God to be able to help you. I understand the spiritual warfare. The enemy will try to make you miss out on what God's trying to do.

Part IV

Offense-Free For Life!

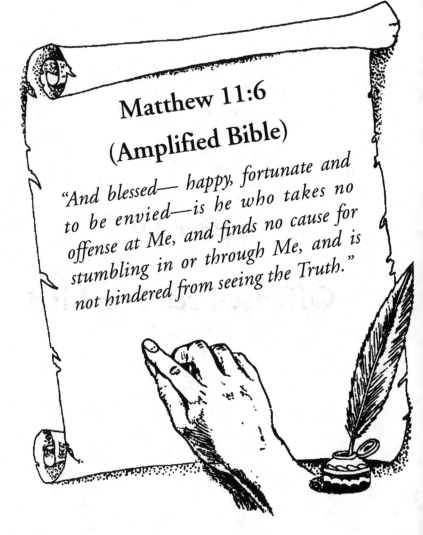

Matthew 11:6
(Amplified Bible)

"And blessed— happy, fortunate and to be envied—is he who takes no offense at Me, and finds no cause for stumbling in or through Me, and is not hindered from seeing the Truth."

Nine Guidelines For Living Life
Free From Offense

I want to give you nine guidelines that you need to follow to keep yourself from getting offended and lead an offense-free, abundant life.

Number One: Keep yourself focused on your purpose or your vision and not on the offense. What can happen is that you can concentrate more on what the person did to you and become sidetracked from what you've been called to do. Keep yourself focused on your purpose. What has God called you to do? What are you desiring to do? Don't let anyone sidetrack you. Don't let anyone throw you off course.

"Ye did run well; who did hinder you that ye should not obey the truth?" Galatians 5:7

In other words, as the Greeks say, *"Who cut in on you and caused you to stumble?"* Who did you allow to hinder you from being able to go forth? When you start obsessing about an offense, you are out of focus, and you're not fulfilling the purpose that God has for you.

91

Number Two: Let the fruits of the spirit have the perfect work in your life. Every day pray. Say, *"Father, thank you for the fruits of the spirit that I have in my life. I want the fruits of the spirit, that temperance, that kindness, that goodness, and that love to be a perfect work in my life."*

Number Three: Keep yourself holy. Live right. You know you are more apt to get offended when you're not living right. So live right. Live holy.

Number Four: Pray the Word regularly. Pray the word regularly and pray in the spirit regularly. You know, every failure in your life is a prayer failure. Believe me, because when you are praying and you're hooked into God, you're being energized, fortified and edified. You're being built up. You're not easily offended when you are spending good, quality time in prayer.

Number Five: Be quick to forgive. Always be ready to release your offender.

Number Six: Make a quality decision to walk in the love which is God's supreme power.

Number Seven: Choose to believe the best, not the worst. Be positive and not negative. Reject those thoughts that offend you. Cast down imaginations.

Number Eight: Ask God to help you with the offense when it comes. Sometimes there will be offenses that you cannot deal with and you're going to need help from God.

Number Nine: Recognize that satan is trying to get you offended. Recognize that he's always working on trying to get you offended.

> *"Great peace have they which love thy law: and nothing shall offend them."*
>
> Psalms 119:165

A Daily Prayer

Father God, I hold my hands up before you and I make a declaration that I will from this day forward walk free from offenses. Jesus, you've already delivered me from them; therefore, I receive that deliverance in my life right now in Jesus' name. Do you hear me satan? Jesus is my deliverer; therefore, I will not receive any more offenses in my life. I say, every, every, every offense is under my feet and whom the son has set free, is free indeed. I'm free. I'm free. Thank God almighty. Free from that bitterness, free from that anger, free from that torment, free from all those things that the enemy brings, again, I'm free! Glory to you, God.

Be Blessed, Happy And Fortunate

"And blessed is he, whosoever shall not be offended in me." Matthew 11:6

Blessed is that man or woman who is not offended in Him. That door is not open for the enemy to attack them and to rip them off. He said, ***"Blessed is he who is not offended in me."***

"And blessed—happy, fortunate and to be envied—is he who takes no offense at Me, and finds no cause for stumbling in or through Me, and is not hindered from seeing the Truth."
Matthew 11:6 (Amplified Bible)

Jesus is talking about himself. If people get offended at Jesus, then they'll get offended at anything.

Let's read what Jesus said one more time. He said, *"And blessed—happy, fortunate and to be envied—is he who takes no offense at Me, and finds no cause for stumbling in or through Me, and is not hindered from seeing the Truth."* Jesus used the words blessed, happy and fortunate; you are to be envied if you can walk free from offense.

Jesus understood the spiritual warfare of the enemy to attack the saints with offense. And he was telling them, you will be blessed if you walk free from offense because I tell you the truth. The Bible says, *"The truth shall set you free."*

I want to be the one who Jesus is talking about right there—blessed and happy. Because do you know what? You're not happy when you've been offended. If you're not happy, you will see the bitterness in yourself. You know what I'm talking about because you've been angry, or bitter, or upset with somebody. The enemy will work overtime to trip you up and stop you from receiving your miracle.

Remember the monkey that tried to get the piece of fruit out of the jar? God is trying to bless you and you're nothing but some ignorant monkey.

Do you remember how they catch those monkeys? They put something the monkey wants in a jar where he can get his hand in. The monkey grabs the goody, holds onto it, and won't turn it loose. He'll just be spitting, kicking, and screaming and they'll just come and get him. He doesn't have sense enough to turn the offense loose. And you're holding onto offenses just like that little monkey. God's trying to tell you to turn that thing loose so you can be set free. God says, turn that thing loose and I can bless you with something else.

Allow God's blessings in your life by taking no offense in our Lord, His servants or His children—our neighbors. You have the tools now to fight with power against the enemy—fight the good fight, and live your life offense-free!